THE PRINCESHIP OF WALES

Series Editor: MEIC STEPHENS

The Princeship of Wales

Jan Morris

First Impression—March 1995

ISBN 1 85902 266 9

© Jan Morris

Printed in Wales by
J. D. Lewis, and Sons Ltd., Gomer Press, Llandysul, Dyfed

'Something must be done', declared King Edward VIII, when he visited the depression-ravaged mining areas of South Wales in 1936. 'You may be sure that all I can do for you I will.' In his youth, after all, he had been presented to the Welsh as their own titular prince. It was as Prince of Wales that he had become famous the world over—Prince Charming come to life, an idol of his day, elegant, handsome and a little racy, as a young prince should be. In the misery of their deprival the people of the coal valleys believed him, and responded with grateful affection. Three weeks later he abdicated, and never set foot in Wales again, or showed the slightest interest in its inhabitants for the rest of his life.

Since the English conquest of Wales, in the 13th century, it had been customary for the heir to the throne to be dubbed Prince of Wales. Edward VIII himself was childless; his successor on the throne, George VI, had only daughters; it was not until 1948 that another male heir was born, to be christened Charles Philip Arthur George and to be created Prince of Wales on his tenth birthday. Three decades on he is still the Prince of Wales, still contemplating his potential destiny as the future Charles III. He is the 18th Prince of Wales under the dispensation of conquest, and he may very well be the last: for while the people of the Rhondda sang hymns for his predecessor, and touchingly accepted Prince Charming's sympathy at the Merthyr Labour Exchange, it is a moot point in the Wales of the 1990s whether there is any point in having a Prince of Wales at all.

How It Happened

There is nothing constitutional, or organic, to the office. When the Anglo-Normans conquered Wales there were no princes in England. Wales on the other hand had been governed by a series of independent and semi-independent rulers who had in recent generations called themselves *tywysogion,* translated by their enemies as 'princes', after the Latin *princeps,* and according to Italian usage—a lesser ruler in medieval Italy, if he had no other titles, was known as *principe*, in effect Chief.

Having defeated the last of the Welsh princes, in 1282, the English symbolically appropriated the title for themselves. In north Wales two years later a son was born to Edward I, the Conqueror, and legend has long maintained that he presented the child to the humiliated Welsh as a proper successor to their native princes, Welsh-born and unable to speak any language that was not their own. Actually this tale was not recorded until 1584, and the boy was not proclaimed Prince of Wales until he was seventeen—and then at Lincoln in England. He really did, however, assume some of the powers, privileges and responsibilities of the dispossessed Welsh princes, and the arrangement gave a veneer of legal authority to the conquest, while acknowledging that Wales was not merely another part of England. This was the first foreign conquest of the Kings of England, the very beginning of the British Empire; although Edward's apocryphal gesture at Caernarfon has gone into English myth as an act of reconcilation, his presentation of a new prince to the people of Wales was really a cynical proclamation of triumph. The Welsh dynasties had been replaced by the House of Plantagenet, and from henceforth the only Princes of Wales would be Englishmen.

In the reign of Edward III, grandson to the Conqueror, it was promulgated that henceforth 'the first-begotten sons of the Kings of England' would be created Princes of Wales. Other kingdoms later copied the idea, and bestowed princely titles upon their royal heirs—the Princedom of Piedmont, for instance, or the Princedom of Asturias in Spain. To this day the best-known of them all, though, has remained the Princedom of Wales. Most people in the world have no notion where Wales is, but many millions have heard of its Prince, and know that he is heir to the throne of England. Not quite every heir, in fact, has been given the title, and a few have never succeeded to the throne—notably the Black Prince, the most formidable of them all. Nor have they all gone on to enjoy successful royal careers: two have been murdered, one disappeared for ever into the Tower of London, one was executed, one died in exile and one abdicated. But some

Kings of England were to be as celebrated as Princes of Wales as they were as Kings—Shakespeare's Prince Hal, for instance, before he became Henry V, the exuberant and influential sybarite who was to become Edward VII, or the discredited Edward VIII himself.

The very first English Princes of Wales did have princely duties to perform, but when Wales was formally annexed to England, by the Act of Union in 1536, they lost all practical function. (The last to be offered an official administrative job in Wales was the future Edward VIII: during the second world war, after his abdication, it was suggested that he might serve as Deputy Regional Commissioner there, but in the event he went more appropriately to the Bahamas). The title itself is purely honorary, and not really hereditary. It is a sort of life peerage, though it does not give its holder the right to sit in the House of Lords. The heir to the throne of England becomes Duke of Cornwall at birth— genetically, as it were—but he has to be *created* Prince of Wales by his father or mother. If a first-begotten son dies before coming to the throne, the second-begotten son does not succeed to the title: and when, as the 1910 edition of the *Encyclopedia Britannica* tells me (later editions have rather lost interest), a Prince of Wales succeeds to the crown, 'the principality in all cases merges at once with the Crown, and can have no separate existence again except under a fresh creation'.

An Abstract Dignity

So it is a somewhat abstract dignity, coming and going, and more abstract still because it has no genuine territorial meaning. As Dukes of Cornwall the heirs to the British throne acquire vast Cornish possessions and responsibilities: as Princes of Wales they acquire nothing but a transient title. Royal apologists like to emphasize the blood-links between the House of Windsor and the Welsh House of Tudor, but in truth there is nothing remotely Welsh about the royal family. 'The maddest Nazi geneticist', it has been said, 'viewing the pedigree of the Queen of England, would hardly oblige her to stitch a red dragon to her hacking-jacket'. The definition of Wales as a 'Principality' is one far more often used by English people than it is by the Welsh themselves, some of whom visibly shudder at the sound of it, and royal visits to Wales have seldom been made for pleasure.

It is hardly a country to appeal to rich and worldly cosmo-politans. Much of the Welsh aristocracy deserted the country centuries ago, and Wales has never been a fashionable sort of place. Its reputation in England has generally been dour or priggish, its temper has been traditionally radical—it was a measure of Edward's popularity in 1936 that he was so able to win the trust of the profoundly socialist Welsh miners. The Crown has few properties here. Even the Anglican Church of Wales was disestablished in 1920, becoming the Church in Wales instead, and leaving the monarchs no responsibility to defend its faith. There are no vast grouse-moors for patrician or plutocratic excursions, no deer-forests, few magnates or tycoons to throw house-parties or arrange balls, not many smart night-clubs or restaurants to be photographed at. Wales is mostly a poor country. Its climate is notoriously awful, its landscapes are demanding, and in the few decades when it found wealth, the profits showed themselves chiefly in blackened valleys, bleak terraced villages and arriviste tycoons few English gentlemen would care to associate with. Its language, tenaciously sustained through so many centuries of English domination, is particularly incomprehensible to outsiders, and as every Englishman tells his friends when he gets home again, the minute you go into a pub they start jabbering away in it.

The English Princes of Wales, then, generally had little to do with Wales. The future Henry V was born at Trefynwy, Monmouth—'all the water in Wye', Shakespeare's Fluellen assured him, 'cannot wash your Majesty's Welsh plood out of your pody'. The future Henry VII, founder of the Tudor dynasty, was born at Penfro, Pembroke, and his son the future Henry VIII is said to have been Welsh-speaking. None of the others could be thought of as Welsh, and probably none would want to be. In the 19th century the royal family, fired by the Mendelssohnian

Queen Victoria, fell enthusiastically out of its mostly German background upon the firs, feudal traditions, fervent royalism and colourful hospitality of Scotland, but none of its members ever acquired a home in Wales (the only modern royal resident has been the crackpot Queen Elizabeth of Romania, the poet Carmen Sylva, who improbably spent five weeks at the Marine Hotel, Llandudno, in 1890). The English upper-classes generally derided and distrusted the people of Wales, and there is no reason to suppose that the royal family felt otherwise. 'Prinny', the future George IV, might perhaps have enjoyed visiting Thomas Johnes's Picturesque folly of Hafod Uchtryd, but can one imagine the future Edward VII, the First Gentleman of Europe, finding satisfaction in Penarth society, or among the rough-and-ready Teifi squires? Or the pedantically proper George V, who became Prince of Wales at the age of 36, coping with life in Ynys Môn, say, with only a solitary Marquis and a hedge-baronet or two to provide suitable company on a pheasant shoot?

For several centuries nobody pretended otherwise. The English Princes of Wales were just that: English princes, with an honorific linking them in a purely formal way with the little-known and hardly comprehensible subject nation to the west. They generally preferred to have nothing to do with the place.

Changing the Relationship

In the 19th century a revival of Welsh national feeling began to change things rather. There were times in the Victorian century when Wales seemed to be going the way of Ireland, that ungrateful traitor to the blessings of British imperialism. Home Rule for Wales was a living issue, and was supported by the powerful Liberal Party against the unyielding opposition of the Tories. William Gladstone, the Liberal leader, who lived at Hawarden in Clwyd, became a Welsh national hero, his portrait to be seen beside those of varied ecclesiastical and educational champions in cottage parlours across the country—for he was not only polit-ically sympathetic, but unlike the raffish and over-fed Prince of

9

Wales of the day (the future Edward VII) was also a devout evangelical Christian.

The movement Cymru Fydd, Wales Will Be, was an active equivalent of Ireland's Sinn Fein, Ourselves Alone. The ubiquitous chapel sects, which had long replaced the Anglican church as the real national faith, were assertively Welsh. Welsh activists set about creating national institutions of their own, altogether distinct from England, sustained by the still predominant Welsh language and by the idealist notion of y *werin,* 'the folk', the dream of a class-less society of profoundly religious and well-educated equals. The University College of Wales was financed chiefly by popular subscription—'by the pennies of the cottage parlour', as the romantics claimed. The peripatetic *Eisteddfod Genedlaethol,* the National Eisteddfod, founded by eccentric litterateurs at the start of the century, became a grand national occasion, with pageantries that were almost State symbolisms. Nationalism in a political sense became a serious issue, as it had never been since the rebellion of Owain Glyndwr in 1404. Its principles were essentially egalitarian, its morality was non-conformist and often pacifist, it voted Liberal and it was disturbing to the supporters of the Established order in London.

The most brilliant of the Welsh politicians was David Lloyd George. Born as it happened in Manchester, he grew up in humble Welsh-speaking circumstances in Gwynedd, and became early in life a self-proclaimed spokesman for y *werin.* He set ominous precedents by winning his first parliamentary election, so he said, as 'a cottage man', fighting the local English or Anglo-Welsh landlords with an almost Irish fury. He was the perfect Welsh leader for the times, anti-imperialist, passionate, chapel-going, a mesmeric orator. It was above all as a Welshman that he was always known in England—'the Welsh Wizard', 'the Welsh Bard', 'the Merlin of Politics', or as John Maynard Keynes put it, 'a half-human visitor to our age from the hag-ridden magic and enchanted woods of Celtic antiquity'. He was the first Welshman since the Cecils of Gwent, in Elizabethan times, to achieve such fame and influence in London.

But he was a man of limitless ambition, and it soon became clear to him that Wales offered too narrow an arena for his talents. He is said to have seen the light during a political meeting at Newport, Casnewydd in Gwent, in 1895, when arguing the case for Home Rule he found himself howled down by his audience of business people. 'We've had enough of all this Welsh business!' cried one of the more vociferous of the burghers, and Lloyd George took note. He rose to political prominence just as the British Empire reached the summit of its power and self-esteem, governing a quarter of the world and nearly a quarter of all its people, and he would have been less than human if he did not feel that it offered more satisfying scope for his political genius than did the aspirations of a half-indigent nation of a couple of million souls that did not even govern itself.

He came to recognize Wales as no more than a small if essential unit of that immense entity—Welsh coal and steel, after all, produced much of the imperial energy—and his bookplate showed a river winding away from the pastoral calm of Gwynedd towards London's triumphal sun. He knew he was destined to play a great part in the imperial drama, and in the event he became its star: Prime Minister of Great Britain at a moment when the British Empire was the most powerful political construction on the face of the globe. Only a minority of Welsh patriots blamed him for abandoning the nationalist cause, most people viewing with pride his progress to the summit of the world: and so, all in all, it was hardly surprising that he more than anyone else gave a new meaning to the hitherto largely disregarded Princedom of Wales.

A Bold Device

Edward Albert Christian George Andrew Patrick David, eldest son of King George V, was created Prince of Wales by his father on his 16th birthday, in 1911. Although he was generally known in the family by his Welsh Christian name, David, he knew little about Wales, and his mother and father had seldom been there either.

Lloyd George was then Chancellor of the Exchequer in Herbert Asquith's Liberal Government, and it was a sign of his remarkable influence, even at the heart of the English Establishment, that the idea was conceived of a grand investiture, in Wales, to introduce the Prince to his nominal subjects. This was a bold and very Lloyd Georgian device. There had never been such a ceremony before. The English Princes had simply been created Princes, and that was that: if there was any ritual involved, it was conducted behind palace doors. Lloyd George obviously saw political advantages in ceremoniously binding Wales more closely to the Crown and thus to the United Kingdom, at once pleasing his constituents at home and mollifying his critics in England. The King, on the other hand, hoped that humouring the whim might temper Lloyd George's dangerous attitudes towards class, privilege and inherited property—might help him in his difficult dealings with the man, as His Majesty implied to his son the Prince. Probably only political expediency could have persuaded a reluctant royal family to submit themselves to such a trumped-up jamboree of sovereignty, and at that time the name of political expediency was written above all in Welsh. Lloyd George himself stage-managed the show, paradoxically assisted in his designs by the (dis-established) Bishop of Asaph, for years one of his fiercest conservative enemies.

Lloyd George held the office of Constable of Caernarfon Castle, which stood within his Parliamentary constituency, and he suggested that the ceremony should be held there. The symbolism would be all too obvious. It was at Caernarfon, so legend perhaps apocryphically said, that Edward I had presented his son to the Welsh chieftains in the first place, and the castle itself was a deliberate expression of imperialism in stone. It was modelled in part upon the walls of Constantinople, and it was intended to set a grand seal upon the English conquest of Wales, as the seat of the royal administration. It had remained the property of the Crown since its construction, and although it never did become a royal palace, and in fact nothing much had ever happened in it, still romantic royalists both Welsh and English liked to associate the building with the English monarchy. Twenty years before, Lloyd George would scarcely have been considered one of them, but in politics twenty years is a very long time.

The ceremonial of the affair was supposed to be based upon Edward I's original presentation of his son, fortified by accounts of the investiture of the future Charles I at Whitehall Palace in 1616, and by evidence from the antiquarian Thomas Fuller, who wrote in 1642 that the 'particular rites of investiture' of the Princes of Wales, extant since the Middle Ages, were 'the Crownet, and ring of gold, with a Rod of Silver'. It was enormously successful. Astutely combining some of the colour of the National Eisteddfod with the mumbojumbo of English royalty, Lloyd George and the Bishop contrived to make the event an allegorical expression of loyalty: the Prince swearing fealty to his sovereign the King of England, the Welsh, chieftains and *gwerin* alike, paying homage to their suzerain. All were pledging their devotion too as subjects of the greatest Empire the world had ever known.

The scene went into the folk-lore of Wales. Almost the entire royal family arrived in State in Caernarfon, guarded by mounted troopers of the Household Cavalry. Within the castle walls 7,000 of the grandest Welsh gentry and bourgeoisie were proud to be greeted and presented to Their Majesties by that notorious agitator and man of the people, David Lloyd George, wearing a plumed hat and a sword. Outside, the narrow streets of the town were crowded with flag-waving citizens in their Sunday best, hatted and gloved, townspeople, quarry families from the slate hills, farmers and their wives. They waited in particular for the moment when the young prince would be introduced to his people by his royal father, fulfilling the ancient legend of Edward I and his baby so long before. This was to take place at Queen Eleanor's Gate, at the east end of the castle, and the local quarry-owner Sir Charles Assheton-Smith carried his enthusiasm so far as to demolish three perfectly good Georgian houses in order to give people a better view.

The vast and terrible fortress (bigger, Dr Johnson once wrote, that he ever supposed a building could be) blazed with flags,

13

velvets, golds and embroideries of monarchical import, many of them especially designed by the Welsh sculptor Goscombe John, R.A. Trumpeters blew fanfares. Beefeaters paraded with halberds. Heralds read proclamations. On display were all the plumes, ribbons, medals, swords, ermines, sashes and buckled shoes of the English Establishment and its Welsh acolytes. The unfortunate princeling, who thought the whole affair rather preposterous, wore white satin breeches and a mantle of purple velvet edged with ermine. Winston Churchill the Home Secretary read aloud his princely titles, and his father the King then adorned him with the baubles Fuller had enumerated: the Coronet, the gold ring, the silver staff. To the Mayor of Caernarfon he rehearsed the lines the Welsh Wizard had taught him: *Diolch fy nghalon i hen wlad fy nhadau*, 'thanks from my heart to the old land of my fathers', followed by the somewhat bathetic afterthought *Môr o gân yw Cymru i gyd* —'All Wales is a sea of song'. Finally, flanked by the King and Queen, attended below by armoured horsemen and behind by a choir of 200 Welshwomen in steeple-crowned hats, he was presented to the populace at the Queen's Gate.

Nearly everyone loved it. It was to the taste of the times, not least in Wales. For years pictures of the occasion graced Welsh houses, especially of course the homes of those privileged to have taken part in the ceremonial—the landed and aldermanic classes in particular. The King and Queen look stiff but satisfied in these remembrances, the future Prince looks understandably selfconscious, the massed ranks of courtiers and soldiers look as though the Empire itself has fallen upon Caernarfon, and unmistakeably at the heart of it all exuberantly stands David Lloyd George, the cobbler's ward from Llanystumdwy. Caernarfon Castle, wrote an official panegyrist long after the event, had at last witnessed a ceremonial worthy of its splendour: 'for the first', said he confidently, 'but surely not for the last time'.

He was right there, for within the lifetime of some of those at Caernarfon that day it was to happen all over again.

For half a century nothing much befell the Princeship of Wales. Edward held the title until his brief accession to the throne, in 1936, and at least kept it in the headlines with his world tours, his ceremonial appearances and his gossip-column gallantries. Otherwise it might almost have fallen into disuse. Two world wars were fought. The British Empire declined towards extinction. Within Wales nationalist feeling variously faltered and revived. The Liberal Party, which had done so much to sponsor the Welsh revival, squabbled disastrously among itself; the people turned overwhelmingly to Labour to see them through the anguish of the Great Depression. Two kings came and went, and a Queen became Sovereign of Britain and of the British Dominions beyond the Seas, what was left of them. Caernarfon Castle dreamed the years away as a tourist spectacle and the home of a regimental museum, unvisited by members of the royal family from one decade to the next. For 22 years, between 1936 and 1958, there was no Prince of Wales at all.

Then Queen Elizabeth's eldest son Charles was granted the title. It was a new Wales whose titular suzerainty he assumed. The coal industry was in terminal decline, soon to deprive the country of its chief source of wealth. The Labour Party, with strong seams of Marxism in its fabric, was all-powerful. The Welsh language seemed to be languishing, the proportion of Welsh-speakers having fallen in each successive census. But Welsh patriotic feeling was, if not perhaps so universal, if anything sharper than it had been. The threat of violent subversion, on the Irish model, was again in the minds of Welsh activists and of British officialdom. A militant youth movement, Cymdeithas yr Iaith Gymraeg, fought bravely for the language. Plaid Cymru, the Party of Wales, was waging a constitutional battle for self-rule. Welsh nationalism had taken on a more overtly anti-English tone, and all the excitement of the world-wide student protest movement was channelled in Wales into passionate defence of the language and the national identity.

For some, then, it was a slap in the face, for others a reassurance, when in 1969 it was announced that the 21-year-old Prince Charles, like his unhappy predecessor, was to be invested in the office of Prince of Wales at Caernarfon Castle on July 1. A Labour Government was in power, and this revival of the past must have been something of a gamble. Rather as in 1911, it was doubtless intended partly to up-stage the nationalist appeal, to infuse Welsh patriotism with unifying royalist sentiment, and to demonstrate that socialists could be just as loyal to the Crown as conservatives. But nobody really knew how well it would work. Was the balance of Welsh patriotism still on the side of the monarchy, or would the shenanigans at the castle inflame separatist feeling, rather than appease it? The previous victim of an investiture viewed the arrangements with a mordaunt eye from his exile as Duke of Windsor in Paris. Not only was he of the opinion that such 'outmoded rituals' of royalty were on their way into limbo, but he still smarted from the suspicion that in 1911 he himself had been no more than 'the pawn of a politician's stunt'.

The arrangements this time were to be masterminded by the young Anglo-Welsh photographer Anthony Armstrong-Jones, created Earl of Snowdon upon his marriage to Charlie's Aunt, Princess Margaret, nine years before. He was Constable of the castle now, and it was doubtless hoped that he would give the ceremony a more indigenous and youthful appeal. The Prince was not obliged to wear the fancy-dress that had so embarrassed his predecessor in 1911, instead assuming his uniform as Colonel-in-Chief of the newly-formed Royal Regiment of Wales, with an ermine cape over it, while Lord Snowdon devised for himself a livery that would have done well for a chorus-line in an Astaire musical of the 1940s, its green barathea, so newspaper readers were told, matching the specially-woven investiture carpets. The theatrical designer Carl Toms was brought in to give the castle a more cinematic aspect; his centre-piece for the setting was a Perspex canopy supported by four steel tubes, said to be the largest Perspex structure ever made (and suggesting to me in hindsight a forerunner of John Paul II's Popemobiles). Welsh singers, composers and poets were recruited too, and much was made, if only heraldically, of the links between the English Princes of Wales and the native princes of old—a banner especially prepared by the Royal College of Arms was alleged to display the arms of Hwfa ap Cynddelw and Marchudd ap Cynan, magnificos as remote to most Welsh people as they doubtless were to the Prince himself.

The London, Liverpool and Cardiff press, then still in the full flush of royalist sycophancy, were ecstatic about the prospect. 'A Great Day for Britain!', cried the *Liverpool Daily Post* in its commemorative souvenir issue. 'Caernarvon's Great Day of Royal Pomp', said the *Daily Express,* dispatching the staff of its William Hickey gossip column to report on the tittle-tattle around the castle. The heralds of the College of Arms were much in demand. Somerset Herald declared in *The Times* that Homage and Fealty were a Living Tradition, while Wales Herald Extraordinary, who had been especially appointed for the occasion, assured his Welsh readers that Prince Charles was descended from two daughters and two sisters of Owain Glyndŵr himself. Much of the ceremony would be bi-lingual, it was emphasized. Most of the invited guests would be Welsh worthies from across the Principality.

Not The Same

Still, it was not the same. In 1911 the Liberal Government could be reasonably sure of a huge loyal majority in Wales, proud of the Empire, devoted to the Crown. In 1969 the Labour Government was faced with a ferment of nationalist activity in Wales, a separatist party which seemed to pose a real threat to the unity of the kingdom, and a powerfully hostile youth movement. Few young Welsh-speaking people cared twopence for royalist tradition, and their own minstrel-prince, the poet-singer-politician Dafydd Iwan, heralded the investiture with a hilariously satirical song, *Carlo,* making merciless fun of Charles and all he stood for. The

17

members of Cymdeithas yr Iaith were waging a furious campaign for the restoration of Welsh place names, very soon to change Caernarvon to Caernarfon even in official documents: the soapily royalist Secretary of State for Wales, George Thomas, an old South Walian Labour stalwart, was their epitome of an Uncle Tom.

Political dissent was in the air. On the very day of the investiture six young Welshmen were sentenced in Abertawe, Swansea, for their activities with the Free Wales Army, a shadowy (and as it turned out ephemeral) instrument of subversion: the judge said of them that they were 'not the only people with ideas of violence in their heads in this land of Wales'. There were denunciations of the investiture as a political device, as a waste of money, as a gratuitous historical insult to Welsh patriotism. In London *The Times,* in those days the acknowledged organ of the Establishment, recognized that all was not as it had been in 1911. What was intended as an occasion for festivity, it admitted, had become a point of controversy. Instead of bringing the countries of the United Kingdom closer the investiture 'seems to have brought forth recrimination and the sad bitterness of rejected good will'. This article the newspaper printed both in Welsh and in English. The English version was headlined NATIONALISM GIVES WAY TO OCCASION—BUT DEEP FEELINGS REMAIN. The Welsh version, perhaps contributed by a Fifth Columnist in the office, read: Y CLEDDYF YN Y WAIN DROS DRO—OND HEB GOLLI MIN (The Sword in the Scabbard for the Time Being—But without Losing Its Edge).

I was in Caernarfon for the event, and I remember the atmosphere as being curiously ambiguous. The town was *en fête*, of course, the castle was beflagged, apparently enthusiastic crowds lined the street—a quarter of a million strong, the papers claimed, not to mention the invisible crowds of 500 million said to be watching on television screens around the world. It was a strange thing to see the familiar faces of world statesmen and politicians peering from the windows of buses as they were driven to the fortress gates, and even stranger to hear the clip and clank of cavalry. Yachts and a warship or two lay off-shore. Jet fighters flew above. Children and old ladies waved Union Jacks, many veterans of two world wars proudly wore their campaign medals. Trumpets sounded from castle towers and elaborate processions conveyed first the Queen, then the Prince, through the streets to the castle, attended by every kind of loyal minion, from Gold Stick in Waiting to the Archdruid of Wales.

But as was said by the Welsh correspondent of *The Times*, Trevor Fishlock, there was 'the sniff of tension' about. Security was overwhelming, enforced not just by uniformed policemen and soldiers, but by plain-clothes-men and intelligence agents everywhere, and through all the panoply of loyalty sounded expressions of dissent. There was an explosion at a nearby railway siding. Students in Maes y Castell, Castle Square, sang Dafydd Iwan's *Carlo*. Somebody threw an egg at the Queen's landau ('Lynch him!' cried the crowd nearby, if we are to believe the papers). There was a palpable heightening of alertness when the Prince, carrying his trinkets of office, appeared with his mother at Queen Eleanor's Gate, watched at relatively close quarters from the site of Sir George Assheton-Smith's still un-replaced terrace.

In fact nothing very revolutionary happened in Caernarfon that day. Welsh nationalists hated it all, of course, and Plaid Cymru declined to have anything to do with it; but the crowds were generally amiable and most ordinary Welsh citizens, I suspect, quite enjoyed it. For the most part they were no less royalist than their fellow-citizens in England and Scotland; certainly nobody was more loyal to Crown and Throne than the throng of the socially privileged who were invitees to the ceremony, and whose special chairs of wood and red plastic, embellished with the Prince of Wales feathers, were sold to them afterwards at £12 apiece, to be seen in the corners of respectable drawing-rooms for ever after. But though it was said to be a shot in the arm for Welsh tourism, though Prince Charles spoke his lines in commendable Welsh, though the Welsh Establishment was enthusiastic about it as the English, though Willliam Mathias composed music for it, and Geraint Evans sang, and Cynan the Archdruid wrote a poem and processed in his robes before the Prince, with 34 representatives of Welsh Youth following behind—still it was not the same. It was a contrived festivity, nothing to do with the living heart of Wales. In the evening I was taken as a guest to one of those yachts off-shore, where we indulged in the pleasures conventional to off-shore yachts, like drinking champagne, and eating cucumber sandwiches, and waving to people in other yachts, and curtseying to Princess Margaret. It gave me a strange feeling to stand upon the deck and look over the water to the great castle, the most fearful of all symbols of the English conquest, built specifically to keep the Welsh in their place by force, and now perpetuating that dominance in more subtle ways.

But even as I watched there, on the road to Abergele in the east two young Welshmen died when the bomb they were carrying, intended to blow up a dam in the name of Welsh independence, prematurely exploded and made martyrs of them both.

Trying His Best

On the whole, I suspect, the British Establishment, like the Labour Government, considered the 1969 investiture a success, but it was never to lodge itself in the Welsh national consciousness, like the 1911 bean-feast. One seldom sees pictures of it in shops or cafés, even in Caernarfon. Contemporary history books hardly mention it (though John Davies, in his magisterial *Hanes Cymru*, does record that it gave Labour politicians a chance to fawn upon members of the royal family). The ceremonies went off well enough, despite that egg on the landau, and certainly it all helped to make Prince Charles better-known in Wales than any English Prince of Wales before him.

Throughout the 1960s, 1970s and 1980s, in periods of Tory as of Labour rule, Welsh resentments stirred and bubbled. Plaid Cymru was having its first successes in Parliamentary elections, and the language movement was unremitting, giving warning to successive London Governments that the threat of Welsh nationalism was not to be disregarded. Sometimes they responded by concessions. A Welsh Office was set up in Cardiff, as a kind of

20

Governorate General, and some of the forms of nationhood were honoured—stamps with dragons on them, pound coins with leeks and Welsh inscriptions. The claims of the Welsh language to legal equality were partially and begrudgingly acknowledged. Under passionate pressure a Welsh-language television channel was sanctioned.

And through it all, for a quarter of a century, it was fondly if intermittently hoped that Charles Philip Arthur George would be accepted by the Welsh people as a true symbol of union and conciliation. He really seemed to do his best for his employers, too. He lacked the charisma of his predecessor in the job, but look where that had led Prince Charming! Before his investiture he spent a term at University College, Aberystwyth, braving the contumely of the more nationalist students, and there he learnt something of the Welsh language and its literature, impressing his tutors as willing and intelligent. Sometimes there was talk of buying a house for him in Wales and making him a resident Viceroy, especially when in 1981 he married his elegant and extremely English Princess Diana.

It would certainly be wrong to say that during those years he was unpopular in Wales, still less rejected. As a lifelong republican myself, on the day of his colossally publicized wedding I dashed off a letter to the Editor of *The Times* objecting to the vulgarity of the monarchical system, and ran away to a nationalist counter-event: a rally at Mynydd Carn in Dyfed, where one of the seminal battles of the Welsh dynastic wars had been fought just 800 years before. It was rather an obscure anniversary—I suppose nobody could think of anything better—and my fellow-demonstrators were fairly few. The day was drizzly, the mountain bare. We huddled up beside the rocks for half an hour or so, exchanging mutually self-congratulatory seditious sentiments, before hastening down the slope to the comfort of our cars: and I could not help feeling some sense of rejection, to have been shivering up there with our principles while almost all the rest of the Welsh nation, together with the citizens of half the world, had been snuggled around their televisions oohing and aahing at the royal spectacle in London.

But then while we were expressing, however limply, a political conviction, our fellow-citizens were for the most part enjoying the sensations of a romantic novel. They were hardly expressing loyalty, as they watched the fairytale performance from Westminster Abbey. Perhaps some of them, every now and then during the nuptials, thrilled to the fact that in title at least the bride and groom were their very own—the Prince and Princess of Wales. They must have been very few, though. The nature of the ceremony was entirely English, its allusions were all to the glory of the English past, and it was above all as heir to the still majestic throne of England that Charles Albert Edward George, wearing his crownlet, went to the altar with his patrician English bride. The very phrase 'Prince of Wales' had lost most of its local meaning by then: wherever I wandered in the world of the 1970s and 1980s, foreigners spoke to me of Dylan Thomas, Richard Burton, Tom Jones or (if it was a rugby country) J.P.R., but I don't remember a single person associating Prince Charles with my homeland.

A Matter of Habit

So as a matter of habit, or perhaps instinct, for 20-odd years after his investiture the people of Wales accepted without general dissent Prince Charles's status as their titular suzerain. For most people, especially younger people, the title seemed to have no political connotations. It came off the tongue without much meaning. Male voice choirs belted out 'God Bless the Prince of Wales' (words by the English balladeer George Linley, c.1841) just as a rousing tune, not a hymn of loyalty—more like 'Bless This House' than 'God Bless America'. From time to time the Prince himself, or his advisers, appeared to remember that there was in fact a political significance to his elevation—he was the symbol, so the theory ran, of Anglo-Welsh union, a marriage consummated by brute force but long since mellowed into general acquiescence. A little touch of Charlie, it was evidently assumed, would quieten the ever-simmering discontent of the nationalists and bring reassurance to the loyalists (not least the thousands of English settlers who were then pouring into Wales in search of easier and cheaper living). Conservative and Labour Governments alike relied upon the royal agency, and no courtier was more assiduous than George Thomas, by now Speaker of the House of Commons, later Lord Tonypandy, who was generally presented to the English as the very archetype of a Good Welshman.

Conscientiously enough the young heir made his statutory visits to his Principality. Brushing up his Welsh, he shook the hands of aldermen and councillors, accepted the flag-wavings of fulsome housewives, chatted up secretaries and jollied along workers—seldom miners now, though, the pits having one by one been closed. Over the years there were few parts of Wales that did not set eyes on him, and only occasionally did unruly students pester him with unfriendly placards. In 1976 he was made Chancellor of the University of Wales, to the consternation of the nationalists and even of some patriots of the old school— the University of Wales, brought into being by the pennies of the *gwerin*, to be headed by an Anglo-German princeling of little scholastic attainment!—and thereafter he was regularly to be seen in academic regalia presiding over degree ceremonies. His two sons were known as Prince William of Wales and Prince Henry of Wales. This was an innovation, I think. The sons of previous Princes of Wales had not adopted such territorial tags— perhaps it was a reminder that the elder of the two was destined one day to succeed his father in the office.

Charles was never more than a visitor, though, generally kindly received but certainly not assimilated. He never did get that house in Wales. He was seldom accompanied by his wife and children. And gradually, as the 'eighties turned into the 'nineties, the Welsh people's perceptions of him shifted. In this they were certainly not alone, and indeed by and large their attitudes towards him were still not very different from that of the English or the Scots. The change was largely a change in the reputation of the monarchy as a whole. The endless shenanigans of the royal family, the successive divorces and separations, the unseemly

23

publicity-seeking, the squabbles overt or suspected, the increasingly frank approach of the Press to matters monarchical—all this meant that the Welsh, like everyone else, viewed the royal family with decidedly less obsequity. For the first time republicanism in Wales became almost a respectable political stance. ('Have you gone mad?' wrote one of my Welsh neighbours when he read that letter of mine in *The Times,* back in 1981.) Prince Charles's welcomes to Wales became noticeably less enthusiastic—as a Sydney newspaper wrote of one of his visits to Australia, 'apathy reached fever pitch'. The last upholders of chapel morality doubtless disapproved of his extra-marital affairs, and I would guess that in his differences with Princess Diana public sympathy was generally with her.

At the same time there was once more a growing sentiment of national feeling in Wales—not perhaps separatism, but at least an urge towards political nationhood of some recognized kind. In 1979, when the Prince was still riding high, the Labour Government somewhat half-heartedly introduced a referendum about devolution; in a depressingly low turn-out the Welsh (and the English inhabitants of Wales) overwhelmingly voted for the *status quo,* the proportion of those who wanted a Welsh Assembly being almost exactly the same as the proportion of those who spoke Welsh. By the 1990s, when a Labour Party in opposition was again proposing devolution, times had greatly changed. The allure of England had faded, the magnetism of Europe had convinced many Welsh people that they would fare better in direct relationship with Brussels, like the devolved provinces of Spain: in 1992 only six out of 38 Welsh MPs were Tories, yet for 15 years the country had been governed by Tory administrations. Successive grudging concessions by London had only induced the activists to press for more, and although by now hundreds of thousands of English people had settled in Wales, the force of the Welsh identity seemed stronger than it had for years.

The Conservative Party in power was profoundly opposed to Scottish and Welsh separatism. Apart from the principle of the thing, anathema to old-school British patriots, their footholds in both countries were tenuous, and truly governing assemblies in both Edinburgh and Cardiff would make Toryism impotent outside England. The faltering prestige of the monarchy, that old instrument of cohesion, must have made them more apprehensive still, and it was hardly surprising that on the 25th anniversary year of his investiture the luckless Prince was once more sent over the border on a propaganda mission. During 1994 he made a series of ingratiating visits, having diligently revised his Welsh once more, in a campaign that was instantly nicknamed 'The Charm Offensive'. Its climax was a ceremony at Caernarfon Castle, where Charles once more pledged himself to the interests of his Welsh people. There was no pretending that this was a wild success. Its style was deliberately muted. No cavalry clattered through the streets this time, no warships lay off-shore, there was only a single fly-past by the Royal Air Force aerobatic team. The Prince wore a nice linen suit. Lord Snowdon had not packed his theatrical Constable's gear. A thousand of the usual dignitaries assembled within the castle walls, bowing and curtseying as always, but the crowds in the streets of Caernarfon were meagre and undemonstrative. Until the police ordered their removal, comical masks of Prince Charles were on sale in the local joke-shop; a satiric poet wearing artificial big ears declaimed disrespectful poetry in Maes y Castell—a performance to horrify the shade of the late Assheton-Smith—and Dafydd Iwan's celebrated lampoon of 25 years before was enthusiastically revived.

Poor Charles! He did his best. He was courteous about the language, complimentary about the catering, observed that music was in the soul of every Welshman and said all the proper things about the goat mascot of the Royal Regiment of Wales. He hoped the anniversary day in Caernarfon would be remembered as a special day for Wales, but the truth is that it will scarcely be remembered at all, and elsewhere too the popularity campaign fell flat. Crowds were small. A rugby crowd at Llanelli was downright flippant. Press attention was off-hand. Even the *Western Mail,* a neo-tabloid which proclaimed itself 'The National Newspaper of Wales' and had generally been fulsomely monarchist, printed the frank headline CHARM OFFENSIVE FAILS, and reported that after nine months of the royal attentions, support for the Prince in Wales had fallen rather than risen. If polls are a true guide, by the end of the year probably most of the Welsh people, whether unionist or nationalist, thought there was little point in having a Prince of Wales at all.

Towards the end of 1994 the *Mail* respectfully ventured to suggest to the Prince that he really did not have the time to be a full-time Prince of Wales. He instantly agreed. 'I am Great Steward of Scotland, Duke of Cornwall, Lord of the Isles, Duke of Rothesay, Earl of Chester, Earl of Carrick and Baron Renfrew. There is also the Commonwealth—and I can't appoint a deputy'. He had other things to think of, too. As Walter Bagehot wrote in 1867: 'All the world and all the glory of the world, whatever is most attractive, whatever is most seductive, has always been offered to the Prince of Wales of the day, and always will be. It is not rational to expect the best virtue where temptation is applied in the most trying form at the frailest time of human life.' The *Western Mail* went on to propose that next time round the *second* son should be made Prince of Wales, leaving the heir to the throne free to pursue his other duties. By then I doubt if many Welsh people cared one way or the other, but various constitutional experts declared such a change perfectly feasible. Two eminent Welshmen consulted were, however, less amenable to the plan. The Conservative Minister at the Welsh Office, Sir Wyn Roberts, thought 'the precedents of history' too strong for it. Dafydd Wigley, Chairman of Plaid Cymru, said simply: 'What I find more interesting is the relationship that will exist between the Prince of Wales and the Welsh Parliament that is certain to be set up before the end of this century.'

A Prince for Wales

Sir Wyn Roberts also made the point that Prince Charles 'had done more for the country than any of his predecessors'. This was not difficult to achieve, but it is fair to say that he has at least shown a benevolent sympathy for the country. His various philanthropic trusts, focussed on the Prince of Wales Committee, have done something for youth and for small businesses in Wales. His interest in the language, whether genuine or politic, has at least persuaded some reactionaries, on both sides of the border, that it is not merely the tongue of cranks and extremists.

But the truth is that however hard he tries, he can never be anything but an English prince from London or from Gloucestershire, viewing his Welsh subjects *de haut en bas* . It is not his fault. Nothing about him is Welsh. He is surrounded by the sort of English aides whose very accents grate and jar upon the ears of all but the most slavishly Anglophile Welsh. For better for worse he represents the English Crown, and as the Crown declines in reputation and allure, so his own prestige in Wales is whittled away. He is far more closely concerned with his immense estates in Cornwall, which have solid financial meaning for him, and it is hard to think that he lies in bed at night thinking about the affairs of Wales: here he is more like an absentee landlord than a socially-conscious squire, and he has no constitutional duties towards his so-called Principality—no Government documents to sign, no policies to approve of.

Let us consider then in what way an English Prince of Wales contributes to the progress and well-being of the nation. Essentially his are the assets of tradition. Standing as he does in succession to the baby Edward II—later found murdered, you will remember, at Berkeley Castle in England, along the road from Prince Charles's estate at Highgrove—he may be said to represent the stability of a Nation-State (though in fact the succession has been nothing if not zig-zag, running as it does through complex lines of affinity from Plantagenets to Tudors to Stuarts to Hanoverians to the House of Windsor). He assembles the loyalties of Welsh royalists, strengthening the bond between Wales and England that has existed since 1282 (though it could be argued that most of the royalists are elderly conservatives, soap-opera sentimentalists or English incomers). He provides a sense of glamour and pageantry (though the glamour has been greatly tainted and the public appetite for pageantry is as easily appeased nowadays by the razzmatazz of show business). His patronage can support good causes (although its effect on the nation through a period of recession seems to have been vestigial). He represents the—well, I was going to say he represents the Moral Certitude which has been a hallmark of the House of Windsor, but not even the most simpering councillor's wife on the green at Caernarfon, limpid before the royal condescension, could still claim that.

In short, for all Prince Charles's good intentions, his office now symbolizes everything that is backward, retrogade and immature in Welsh society: subservience to English rules and manners, a nostalgic harking upon the past, unquestioning adherence to an outdated political system and an insular disregard to the nation's potential as a self-governing member of the European Community. As always, the English Prince of Wales remains not a real prince of Wales at all, but merely a delegate of English supremacy.

This need not be so. Let us suppose ourselves for a moment to be progressive Welsh royalists, if such a flight of fancy is possible, and imagine an ideal English Prince of Wales. For a start he would be, as the *Western Mail* proposed, a full-time incumbent. He would be a Viceroy, the Queen's honorific deputy in Wales, whose duties would embrace all those displays of style and ceremonial that Governors-General preside over in Canada. This would certainly mean coming to live in Wales, and providing a focus of Welsh pride and consequence. Perhaps Cardiff Castle could be made over to the Prince, as a building that is historically neutral, more or less, or perhaps he could acquire a Welsh Highgrove, a country house where he could live in a style suitably Welsh, surrounded by Welsh-speaking staff, honouring Welsh traditions: like Glyndŵr at Sycharth, say—

Na gwall, na newyn, na gwarth
Na syched fyth yn Sycharth..
No want, no hunger, no shame
No one is ever thirsty at Sycharth...

No longer attended by English toffs, nor even by Anglicized Welsh sycophants, there he could create a true centre of Welsh culture, to be emulated all over the country as the ways of princes are. Welsh actors, authors, poets, musicians classical and rock would be familiars there. Welsh scholars and intellectuals and industrialists would often be at the Prince's table. When diplomacy was needed, to ease through a foreign contract, encourage a foreign investment, persuade a foreign conductor to perform at the National Eisteddfod, the name and influence of the Prince of Wales would always be on hand.

When it came to the National Eisteddfod, indeed, the Prince would be modestly in the audience. His white cattle would compete at agricultural shows. He would open exhibitions, distribute prizes, cut ribbons, judge competitions, not as a visiting celebrity but as a citizen of Wales himself. His ample largesse would encourage the language, and he would be a welcome guest if he ever turned up at a meeting of Cymdeithas yr Iaith. All the pomp and subservience of a monarchy in England would be dismissed by this royal satrap in Wales. Bagehot suggested that the power of the Crown depended upon a mixture of mystery and revelation—a private mystery pierced now and then by shafts of theatrical display. The ideal Prince of Wales would realize that in Wales such mystery counts for nothing any more. Just as, for one day, the future Edward VIII made himself seem human and comradely—'Something must be done'—so the perfect English Prince of Wales would present himself above all as a royal fellow-citizen, if not Welsh-born, at least Welsh by adoption and dedication.

How could anyone calling himself the Prince of Wales honestly do anything else? And if he had no time or taste for such commitments, then let him move over, as they used to say in America, and make way for a guy who does.

Prince President

But I am being an advocate for the devil, arguing that there could still at a pinch be a place for an English Prince of Wales. In fact I find it impossible to conceive that any royal scion would be willing to pursue such a dedicated career down here in the sticks with us: and as a republican myself, and an egalitarian, and a Welsh

29

separatist, and a modernist, and a romantic, and a bit of a fantasist, I have a better idea anyway.

'The Welsh', wrote the novelist Cledwyn Hughes in his book *Royal Wales* (1957), 'remain the most Royalist of people . . . we, from Wales, adore the Queen who lives in London Town'. It is perfectly true that royalism and Wales have traditionally gone together. Welsh legends from long before the conquest are full of lofty kings and princes. In the Mabinogion the Prince of Dyfed changes places as an equal with the King of the Underworld, and in the story generally supposed to refer to Caernarfon Castle, the story of Macsen Wledig, the central figure is a Roman-Welsh king—the historical Magnus Maximus, Spanish-born but Welsh-adopted, who was proclaimed an anti-Emperor by his soldiers and was to become a sort of honorary Welsh hero. The Arthurian tales which have played so large a part in the Welsh literary consciousness are nothing if not tales of royalty, replete with courtly chilvalry performed (or so we like to think) in a Welsh setting. One of the earliest of recorded Welsh games was *Tawlbwrdd,* Throwboard, which was played with a team of a King and eight common men *(gwerin),* the King being equal in importance to all the eight commoners put together.

The historical kings and princes of Wales, too, the indigenous rulers who were here before the English came at all, have never been forgotten or downgraded in the national memory. Hywel Dda, the Lord Rhys, the two Llywelyns— they were royal all, and are heroes still. Among Welsh patriots there is a clear distinction between the castles of the Anglo-Normans, like Caernarfon, and the castles of the Welsh princes—real Welsh castles, as it were, representing even in their ruins the identity of an ancient people: if the organizers of those investitures had been more historically sensitive, they might with advantage have mounted them beside the sea at Cricieth, say, or at the desolately dramatic Castell-y-Bere, up the valley from Craig Aderyn, that strange Rock of the Bird where the cormorants nest. The best-loved of all Welsh national monuments is probably Llywelyn's Stone, which stands beside the river Irfon in Powys, near the spot where the last of the hereditary Welsh rulers was killed by English troopers in 1282. *Ein Llyw Olaf,* Our Last Leader, it says upon its plinth, and every year on Llywelyn's Day, December 11, a group of mourners assembles there to remember the terrible day .

The supreme Welsh champion of them all, Owain Glyndŵr, presented himself always as a royal prince, and was accepted by the people as such. At the height of his rebellion in the early 14th century he really did rule virtually all of Wales, and sent his own ambassadors to foreign monarchs. He never did take Caernarfon Castle, but he set up his headquarters in the equally royal fortress of Harlech, where he surrounded himself with the consequence not just of a Government, but of a court. If tradition is true he actually crowned himself Prince of all Wales in a ceremony at Machynlleth in 1404.

No Welsh patriot has ever resented his princely pretensions. To be a prince, if not a king, was his proper condition as the head of a sovereign people, and today even members of the English royal family are not ashamed to claim kinship with the old rebel, though it probably took Welsh Herald Extraordinary to remind them of it. He was the last true Prince of Wales: the last who was really Welsh, the last to consider himself a Welshman always, the last to devote himself to the happiness, the advancement and the reputation of Wales, and its place in the world beyond these islands—they can make an English prince the Prince of Wales, by a stroke of pen on parchment, but they can never make him a true Prince of the Welsh.

I think it possible that embedded in the sub-conscious of even the most radical Welsh person, there is some residual weakness for the idea of princeship, so flamingly embodied by Owain long ago. The English themselves, after all, stole it from the Welsh in the first place, and used the title for nobody but the Prince of Wales until the reign of James I, when for the first time the children of the sovereign were, to coin a verb, emprinced. What better then, when the time of independence arrives, than to dub our own elected President *Tywysog Cymru,* in the line not of Charles and 'Prinny' and the Black Prince and Edward II, but of Glyndŵr and the Llywelyns and all the misty indigenous lords of our past? The functions I outlined a page or two back for an

English princely paragon (or chimera) are in fact exactly the functions one would require of a president—formal, ceremonious, honorific, philanthropic, cultural functions, but unifying functions too, giving the nation a centre of gravity, fostering its self-respect and its wholeness. They are nothing to do with royalty. Eminent and respected citizens, chosen by their peers for the job, could perform such duties with infinitely more distinction and affection than any reluctant cub of the Windsor kennel: what is more, at the end of their fixed terms of office, if they failed to satisfy us we could be rid of them—move over, bud!

The institution of an English Prince of Wales, son to the English monarch, is (to be frank at last) a dead loss. It is meaningless, silly and insulting. The sooner Prince Charles himself accepts the fact—and he must surely be aware of it already—the better for everyone. Most of us would perhaps be sorry, though, to see the end of that ancient title, inherited from Gwynedd and Dyfed, Deheubarth and Dynefor. Adopt it for the Welsh Republic that is sure to come one day, make our head of State uniquely a Prince-President, and the pubs can keep their inn-signs without a blush, the world will recognize a sign of grace and individuality, and even the most passionately anti-monarchist among us will be able to sing (bilingually, of course) a triumphant 'God Bless the Prince of Wales'!